SIBILA PETLEVSKI Soiled With Earth, Drunk On Air

COPYRIGHT © 2025 Sibila Petlevski

The Croatian version of this book was published
under the title *Prljavi od zemlje, pijani od zraka*
(Zagreb: Litteris, 2022).

A choice of poems from this book in French translation
was published in the anthology of world poetry
Anthologie de la poésie mondiale
(Paris: Editions Caractères, 2020).

DESIGN & LAYOUT
Nikša Eršek

PUBLISHED BY
Sandorf Passage
South Portland, Maine, United States
IMPRINT OF
Sandorf
Severinska 30, Zagreb, Croatia
sandorfpassage.org

PRINTED BY
Znanje, Zagreb

Sandorf Passage books are available to the
trade through Independent Publishers Group:
ipgbook.com / (800) 888-4741.

Library of Congress Control Number: 2024952366

ISBN 978-9-53351-527-4

This book is published with financial support by
the Republic of Croatia's Ministry of Culture and Media.

SIBILA PETLEVSKI

SOILED WITH EARTH, DRUNK ON AIR

SAN-
DORF
PAS-
SAGE

SOUTH PORTLAND | MAINE

CONTENTS

Hey, People!, 11
Time Is Born, 12
The Artist, 13
In Vain, 14
A Good Land, 15
Black Magic, 16
Invisible, 17
Accidental Sailing, 18
The Point Of Absence, 19
Thousands Of Faces, 20
Over Time, 21
Obscuration, 22
Mimicking, 23
Second Birth, 24
Hunger, 25
Artificial Leather, 26
Disappearing, 27
Buried Night, 28
Dog's Life, 29
In Service, 30
Space Of Freedom, 31
Signature, 32
I Walk, 33
In The First Light, 34
Buried Together, 35
Pentagram, 36
Anchorage, 37
Melancholy, 38
Labyrinth, 39
Decision Tree, 40
I Suffer, 41
Fire Eating, 42
Keys To Heaven, 43
Coming To A Standstill, 44
Goose-Step, 45

Another Morning, 46
A Lost Breed, 47
Our Lady, 48
Beneath The Foundation, 49
Skin Knowledge, 50
Right Now, 51
The Land Of Centaurs, 52
Sinkholes, 53
A Petal Of The Trinity, 54
Rainmaking, 55
Earthlight, 56
Seduction, 57
In This Hell, 58
Staying On, 59
Delta Formation, 60
Dead Water, 61
The Sacred Hill, 62
Conquest, 63
Doubt, 64
Exception, 65
By Accident, 66
The Face Of The Hunter, 67
The Assumption, 68
For Eternity, 69
Opening The Eyes, 70
Horizon, 71
The Economy Of Beauty, 72
The End Of History, 73
The Herd, 74
Eviction, 75
The Wind Of Experience, 76
Downpour, 77
Child, 78
False Thought, 79
Deaf Mine, 80
Where We Are, 81
Putting Full Stops, 82

The Fear Of People, 83
Black Furrows, 84
Stunned By The Sun, 85
Wind Rose, 86
Hat's Feather, 87
Geometry Of The Night, 88
Together, 89
Ice Age, 90
Slow Melting, 91
Dim Light, 92
Oblivion, 93
Breath-Forms, 94
Money, 95
Ear To The Heart, 96
The Point Of Despair, 97
Bring Back The Blush, 98
I'm Sorry, 99
Jumping Out, 100
Palm Leaves, 101
Smiling Asleep
    I, 102
    II, 103
    III, 104
Stone Children, 105
Curiosity, 106
Form-In-Abandonment, 107
Green Walnut, 108
Wolfsbane, 109
Upturned Skin, 110
The Celestial Tree, 111
Luna Moths, 112
Naked Lady, 113
Blank Slate, 114
The Happy Plant, 115
Horror Plant, 116
Sun Stealer, 117

The Chisel Of Silence, 118
Golden Shower, 119
White Phosphorus, 120
Daisy Heads, 121
Messages Of Heaven, 122
Walled Up, 123
Eternal Love, 124
The Extinction Of Light, 125
Let's Go Home, 126
Poison, 127
The Guardian Of Happiness, 128
Drugged, 129
The Third Eye, 130
Hundreds Of Years, 131
Horizontal Growth, 132
Along The Road, 133
Smoke, 134
Masks, 135
Over The Edge, 136
Desert, 137
Obedience, 138
Glory Of The Snow, 139
The Path Of No Return, 140
What If?, 141
It Falls, 142
War, 143
Eyes Shut, 144
Witnesses, 145
Puzzle Game, 146
A Blood Spiral, 147
Fire, 148
Encounter, 149
The Family, 150
Magical Plant Characters, 153

I am the herb whisperer. My poetry is a libretto for whispering to magical herbs and listening to the voices of silence. Plants are the protagonists of this collection. Its pages make the space after the apocalypse. I started writing it long before the corona madness, long before the chills of the Third War crept into my bones. I wrote these verses during 2019 and 2020. You could say that, in many ways, I predicted the atmosphere of giving up, fear, isolation, and overcoming all of the above through understanding people as part of nature. My verses are material for the ecology of the spirit. Different people from distant parts of the world call the characters from this spiritual drama by different, yet similar, names. Variants are important. Calling is important. People are important. Don't look for the botany in the poem: look for the story in the blank space between the names. Let the magic of herbs take you. This is not environmental poetry: these poems have grown from the soil of your soul. Recognize them in silence. Find me by chance—while you are looking for yourself.

HEY, PEOPLE!

The clouds beg me to recognize
them and say—look, a goose

feather and a bearded face, and
a threatening finger. They ask me

to believe, to climb the serrate leaf
toward the evening sky, and to

count sheep by sheep until I lose
consciousness. And then they

take me as one of them; kneading me
mindlessly between boobs and

choking me with airbag pillows.
Does anyone see me from below?

TIME IS BORN

Letter-shaped balloons emit
air rapidly. In front of the eyes

of a sleepy child learning to
memorize the alphabet

of survival, the green foliage
intoxicated with young blood

twists, dances, and shakes.
The small skeleton—

wrapped in the arms of a
tree—stays upright and

continues to grow: its Time
is yet to come into this world.

THE ARTIST

Balancing on thin stalks
of serenity, sometimes

approaching, sometimes
distancing, we have discovered

a secret: fate uses the wind to
laugh in our faces shamelessly.

The wind is the artist who
creates fear of separation.

The in-between-space
always remains the same.

IN VAIN

If we only knew how to
breathe out the message

to the fire and tell it
our skin was made of air,

it would have embraced us
with cold flames, and we

would be glowing together
now. If we choose to give

life, the earth would
throw us out: the black

greasy earth always
returns what it receives.

A GOOD LAND

Who has taken the face off the man
with the head back, and what factors

influenced the choice of that face from
a pile of rotting Adam's apples thrown

into a ditch by the side of the road?
Who has translated that man's name

into the language of snake grass, and
were the rabbit's ears the last to hear

the way his mother used to call him?
A good land accepts without question.

BLACK MAGIC

Black Adam's ears are
listening to the clatter

of dirty children's feet,
and his underground

tuber, like an apple
with a dead jaw print,

is still afraid of the bite,
and will never be able

to overgrow fear. When,
drunk as hell, I tell him—

stay calm, beloved—
he stops dead in his tracks

and waits for the sky
to come down on us.

INVISIBLE

I am following close
behind the pack

in a slow row down
the slope. Hunger

takes me through
the beech forest.

There is a narrow
trail in the first

snow: paw after
paw, wolf behind

wolf. We are hunting
an invisible doe

together. There is
a rustle in the thicket.

Shivers up the spine:
I am holding my breath.

ACCIDENTAL SAILING

Ribs sticking out
from the keel of

a hollow boat:
morning filling it

with rain. Meadow
butterfly pupae

peeling an old
green paint from

the hull; taking
down larvae to

a dry place and
stacking them side

by side. Fleawort,
a male weed, firmly

anchored to a puddle
with its root,

is able to set sail
only when a bird

accidentally rips off
a bitter leaf

with its beak and
throws it away.

THE POINT OF ABSENCE

Ships have been carrying us
on the shallows for a long

time, the masts have been
keeping our spine erect;

the sails putting white clothes
washed with salt on our

naked and dead bodies.
As gold ballast floats, shells,

strung into a coral reef collar,
outline the neck of Atlantis.

As if giving us an overhaul, they
have been dragging us through

the bottleneck of the story—
straight to the point of absence.

THOUSANDS OF FACES

Rhombus-made script is
the only way a poplar can

say that it is not kindling;
that it is not firewood

for the stake at which our time
burns the bones of its enemies.

No one cuts anything into
the bark of the tree: the bark

itself performs the geometry
of despair proving it on itself.

Thousands of dark faces
in the wind revealing

the whiteness of their
reverse sides with each flicker.

OVER TIME

It can be long hidden
and then one day—

having forgotten that
over time it has reduced

itself to the bare naked
waiting, it can realize

that the thing anxiously
awaited is a ball of

dried weed rolled up
in the desert; a Jericho

head looking for a body,
and a rose that needs no root.

OBSCURATION

The fire, which leaves no wreckages,
disintegrated the night and tightly

entangled the strands of smoke.
I could not avoid meeting my own

shadow, which, larger than me,
briefly soot-painted the plot of land

over which I flew so fast that I could not
immediately realize the effect of

the eclipse produced by the wings
did not change the color of the grass.

MIMICKING

My orchids disguise themselves:
they take on the shapes of

innocent infants, or shake with
the skulls of an extinct tribe, and

then they put on monkey faces
and laugh at themselves; deceive

wasps to swallow them, and gently
flutter with the false wings of the holy

spirit. One day, any superfluous
imitation will serve its purpose.

SECOND BIRTH

Blind worms are slithering
through the grass: they are

my guides, and my hope
born alive from an egg

cracked in the womb, staying
hidden until the second

birth. Sheared-off bark
hissing: baptized in birch

water, I am slowly converting
to another faith, moving

to the other side of the
unknown—drop by drop.

HUNGER

Wild plum trees bleed with
resin. Trunks with stab wounds

fizzle and chirp. Thick orange
juice trickles. Bareheaded baby

birds think the trees are talking
in the language of their hunger.

Only when they are dead, their
beaks will be filled with worms.

Cats have eaten their mother's
tongue. Not even death could

reconnect what has been taken
apart in the dying moments.

ARTIFICIAL LEATHER

Let me tell you what comes before
our entering the vacuum chamber:

the wheat shall undo its braids
and the last wind we could feel

shall blow the grain out of
the unbraided wheat ears. The new

genus shall crucify the artificial
skin, bake a bread, and declare

it has to eat in order to survive.
The Host—when it drops down to

the metal stomach as a small coin
—shall bear witness to the lie.

DISAPPEARING

Our myrtle bush blooms
with wax and every flower is

a hollow hope casting.
The same mold has served us

for years. In the lost wax process—
that over which we pour hot gold

is lost. The tangibility of the void
is comforting. In the void, the taste

of the fruit is surprisingly good:
the flavor of the disappearing Host.

BURIED NIGHT

Endless grass: wherever
the view goes. Under each

thistle in blue bloom, deep
in the meadow—a bat wing.

Buried night always finds
a way out. It does not linger

long in a blind eye full of earth.
Groundwater flushes away

the congealed dark indigo skies
and gives to the root a chance

to choose the color of the flower
that will see the light of day.

DOG'S LIFE

Four black opaque blueberries
seeing through the eyes of

a newborn puppy
who doesn't know it has

two faces. The one that sees
ahead, is chasing tail and

running circles in front of
the nose of the other

that can in no way stop
waving at things

already gone beyond
the horizon of the future.

IN SERVICE

Tied up by the devil's ivy,
we expose the liver to blue birds.

Their beaks fail to penetrate
either the skin or the round

ligament. The golden creeper
hugs us and clutches us close

to the cold wall. First, the rain
washes the stomach, then,

sunbeams, barely squeezed through
the clouds, warm the holiness

of the naked scalp. We serve
to the end: the goal is to fulfill.

SPACE OF FREEDOM

It is scary to reduce the reality
of a tree grounded in a stump

to reading its rings. There is
no fateful number: just a gap

between the rings, which are
denser in the north than in

the south. The tree is not faulty
when a slanting line intersects

the circle. The tree does not sin.
There is no room for freedom in it.

SIGNATURE

Until recently, water peonies
bloomed here, and yellow pistons

crumbled down into the cinnamon
water. Wasps had taken all

the honey from the hives along
with the living bowels of bees.

After the carnage, only the bitter
taste of the stolen remained.

I seek in vain for the signature
of the sweet flag in the sludge.

I WALK

There is a dew of blindness
in my eye. On my tongue—

there is a poison of sandy apples
scattered around the edge of

the lagoon. I don't breathe.
I don't look around. I walk.

As if I was wading through
a cane field swinging the sickle

—that is how I make my way
from dawn to dawn.

IN THE FIRST LIGHT

One wound after another—
dressed with ivy; sores getting

overgrown by leaves with jagged
edges. My eyes, my numerous

eyes, trickling clotted blood into
the lattice—enmeshed in tightly

stretched, heavy layered nets
glowing in the night. Every eye

is looking at its own blind spot.
Poppy heads are beginning to cry

slit open. The blue of the sky is
getting smeared with the wind.

A patch of barren land just starting
to germinate: thorns sprouting

on thorns. The first light of day
begins to suck from my white

veins: lukewarm milk drops
falling down on the sleepy garden.

BURIED TOGETHER

It's not true the collecting
passions of tiny animals, and

their dressed skins, furiously
streaked with lines of experience,

belong to different dimensions
of reality. There is a small

time shift separating them:
such illusions grow inside

the same opium poppy pod,
and stay there, buried together.

PENTAGRAM

Stars have been dripping
into the wine cask all

night long. With my tongue
stuck out—I greeted the liquid

light instead of the dawn,
and thus, I came to know

this brilliant sunrise
is yet another disguised

darkness: a yellow pentagram
of wild tobacco in bloom.

ANCHORAGE

Comet tails getting grounded
in waves of fire. Every tiny

end of days that exceeds
the limit of somebody's pain

is having the wind at its back
while passing by word of mouth.

The moment it looked as if our ark
full or wretches was going to set sail,

the seeds in a deadly nightshade's
black pod, decided to come to rest.

Our destiny is calmly waiting
for us: anchored in a moist mound.

MELANCHOLY

Sometimes, when the nails on
the black claws of mountain ash

begin to bud, a melancholic
mood descends upon us and

our grandmothers' wrinkles
begin to move before our eyes

with the ripple of smiles as if
they were living water. If we are

thirsty, the whole stream fits in
the cup of our hand; if we are

hungry, the wind feeds us with
the smell of a white deer's blood.

LABYRINTH

I'm breathing into a starry cluster,
mouth to mouth with a flower—

right here, were I used to cut mountain
germander with a sharp knife. How

come the maze hovering overhead,
suddenly opens up, right here, where I

used to carry milk, climbing the goat's path
to the cabin? The heart stops paralyzed

by the chloroform: all of time fully fits
into the cochlea of the scalding sky.

DECISION TREE

Possibilities branching off from
the existing line of sight: dried

blood and preserved footprints
of mummified legs. For every mile

of a road there are two miles of
burning bushes housing relics

for veneration. The shape of a holy
bramble engraved into granite

should be read as the letter
of the law. The spirit gets away.

I SUFFER

I did not take off my clothes for fear
that something might threaten

the nonexistent, but the seed would
never have taken root if the earth

had not torn off its armor. Army
backpacks again filled with yarrow

for wounds. I suffer silence so I don't have
to go by the rut of words. When I dive

deep enough, my blood turns ocean
green, and as soon as I put the knife

to my skin, my little world begins
to pour into the bigger one.

FIRE EATING

North wind wipes out
notes made in clean air,

and dull tips of the Himalayan
cedar trees are starting

to lose their hair. Cones are
falling apart while still

attached to the branches.
Hanging stone gardens

mimic the spine of the
mountain covered in snow.

Rocks get broken apart
by an eternal smile. With

every next breath there is
less and less fire to swallow.

KEYS TO HEAVEN

When little drops of sun,
sticky as kisses, wrapped

clouds in colorful clothes
for the last time, people

suddenly wished to put their
heads in them. Never before,

never again. Petty souls
began to nudge the horses

of eternity desperately
with little red spurs. The light

was so joyful that day and
the enlightenment so sad.

COMING TO A STANDSTILL

According to the secret law of the reverse
direction of growth—the ancient branches

of a yew tree had put down roots, while
they were wiping off deadly sweat from

the face of the Earth. The southern wind
hopelessly plays the comb of the grounded

crown: everything has come to a standstill,
and the strongest of all storms is devoid

of any sound. At the invitation of
voiceless trumpets—bodies refuse to rise.

GOOSE-STEP

My days are rolling in the catmint's
fragrance: ecstasy makes nets

at every neglected corner. It is not
a cobweb—that thing my hands get

entangled in—but rather the play
of light: bronze dust in a sunbeam.

Chain links are breaking one after
another, and melted sugar-wool is

dripping loudly to the floor. Red ants
are parading with goose-step all over me.

ANOTHER MORNING

Blue hobbits drink the night
sky. The secret is that they

grow on the tip of the tongue,
like the words of scripture

that none of the unreliable
witnesses — walking the earth

like black bugs armed with
battle cuirasses of faith in death

— have managed to soil with
their thoughts. Let them go

to where they've come from.
In my garden scarabs feed

on grass. The emerald
glow of their shields defends

the truth of my night from
the lies of another morning.

A LOST BREED

Yellow pine needles are stitching
fur skins and lining up the necklace

of mistletoe berries on the umbilical
cord, just for the amusement of

the younglings with bloodstained
tongues. The feeble growling of bear

cubs calling the dawn. Soft paws
walking in circles, leaving in the soil—

still moist with warm entrails—
the footprint of a lost wild breed

more similar to the track of a badger,
than to the track of a beast.

OUR LADY

Happiness, smaller than
a cricket and a hummingbird

hawkmoth, lies on a blanket
of dry yellow spring flowers

pretending to be dead. Our
Lady's nectar proboscis trembles

as she moistens the bedstraw
with muffled tears of joy.

Her inhuman body is outlined
beneath the blue cloak of the sky.

BENEATH THE FOUNDATION

There is a walnut tree here:
its crown leaving no room for

anything else in the backyard
of a vanished house. Black mulberry

root is finding its way below
the roofless foundation. A spider

is teaching a silkworm how to braid
a wreath, and make a cuckoo nest;

how to knit a pair of baby socks,
and weave a white shroud, and

how to draw a thread by using
a hawthorn thorn as a distaff.

SKIN KNOWLEDGE

When a thought comes
to my skin awareness,

I cannot forcibly pull it off
as if skinning a rabbit.

I can't even shed it naturally
like snakeskin: I have to stop,

bury myself in the ground
like a bulb, and wait until

a tulip of a never-before-seen
sky blooms above my head.

RIGHT NOW

I'm listening to the night and
the night—disheveled, ears

rolled into trumpets—is listening
to me. I hadn't even managed

to bite loudly into the black root
of the white hellebore yet, and

my angel had already started scraping
the air with its wings, pouring crumbs

of Paradise into my hands. I'm picking
Lenten roses under the moonlight.

THE LAND OF CENTAURS

The sky has been sown from below.
Crevices are spitting out white safflower

seeds wherever there is a notch made
in the ground to count how much

running water the soil has drunk up.
Mourning doves come flying to witness

the settling of scores. They do not coo,
nor do they peck seeds—they just stand still

in pairs, and their standing proves that
things are as they are: wrongly directed

as a centaur's legs trying to get rid of man
by galloping frantically backward.

SINKHOLES

The acceleration of gravity
is a measure of the speed of

ascent interspersed with
frequent falls into sinkholes

that give me some space
to find my place, to build

a house, to join a settlement
at the bottom. I walk briskly

through puddles, ravines,
and winding clefts in the rock:

my shoes are limestone
potholes overgrown with grass.

A PETAL OF THE TRINITY

I do not leave. Red clover lawns
are moving away from me.

The sun burns marks onto
the grass. On the two of us—

who used to roll in the grass
and laugh out loud—it looks

as if we were branded with
a red-hot iron to identify

the owner. The traits we share,
mother, do not lose color:

they just smell like dried red
clover, and have a scent of a river

saying goodbye to its riverbed;
they smell of earth bidding

farewell to a foot. I stay here
in the name of That which

is not, and does not want to
be a petal of the trinity.

RAINMAKING

Our long hair dragged heavily
in the mud, tightly intertwined

like honeysuckle, luring fish
into the tubes of flowers. Yoked

together, like two sisters, we pulled
the plow over the river silt; lifted

air silver coins from the bottom,
and called for rain with the quail

cry, and with the peek from
the lungs of a young birch tree.

EARTHLIGHT

Satisfied women, having grown
flower beards, kneaded a dough of

grey mud, spreading it with their hips.
A herd of small elephants, smaller

than the palms of their hands, appeared
out of nowhere: their hooves shaping

gouge craters everywhere—making
every hectare of the moonlit estate

resemble a square of the lunar
surface under the earthlight.

SEDUCTION

Luna has left pollen grains
on the doorstep: a yellow

sign that something dead
inside lives again. Angel's

trumpets have spilled poison
on the doorpost. No one is

allowed to enter anymore.
In the lee side, sadness

intertwined with joy crawls
up the wall. The darkness

seduces me in vain.
I don't unravel: I cut.

IN THIS HELL

Pairs of praying mantises,
erect on two feet, holding

hands. Legs of ladybugs
dripping with false blood.

Two stag beetles fighting
with interlaced jaws on

a piece of rotten fruit.
A blue devil in a sun-scorched

field mounting a bayonet
of thorn on every single leaf.

STAYING ON

That body I have found
on a silver river shoal,

deposited like sand and
silt and pebbles—it is no

different from the coast
itself. It looks as if it has

either come out of nowhere,
or has been there forever.

That foreign body, ready
to enter me—like a splinter

stuck under my toenail
—says to me: *stay on.*

DELTA FORMATION

The green one outgrowing itself
slowly—by an inch, by a foot,

by a head. The innocent one
sucking ground; its leaf tapping

on a dry breast of the naked
stone in a karst landscape.

The wild one gnawing
the way for a peaceful river

with its first tooth. The flock
changing direction: pulling

the river delta with the first beak
toward the cove in the skies.

DEAD WATER

We have tied tongue knots
voicelessly. What we wanted

to say, has ended in the darkness
of our mouths: in the tiny weave

of thirst between live roots of red
mangroves and their reflection

in dead water. As if wandering
in the rainforest with no signpost,

—we have lost the thread of
conversation, and who knows

how many more times
we will start all over again.

THE SACRED HILL

Our words are rough to the touch.
We write in the knot alphabet

—so that nothing is forgotten—
and we persistently climb the same

sacred hill, naively carrying a clean
white towel with us to wrap in it

a tuber of silence and a screaming
root of our forcibly grafted beings.

As long as we're together we don't
mind being dead while yet alive.

CONQUEST

A stranger has made a nest
of longing in us, so we began

to steal from huge birds
—wing by wing, setting blood

sails. Our squadron managed
to win hearts filling them

with horror—one after another.
and the whole universe began

to close within itself like a bush
of mimosas: world after world.

DOUBT

I've never been followed
by a single dry leaf with

such a loud rolling sound
before, as if it wanted to

catch up with me on an empty
road in the middle of the day

in the heat of the summer.
This noon is a butterfly with

crumpled wings mimicking a
dead thing scorched by the sun.

I am leaving a trail of doubt
in the dust with my breath.

EXCEPTION

As they rush madly across
the endless meadow sown

with marigolds, every now
and then they stumble, and

as in a minefield, they set off
a chain reaction. Some comfort

each other that it is easier
together. Others hope to be

exempt from the rule, like
a purple mountain star flower

that miraculously found itself
down in myriad orange heads.

BY ACCIDENT

Blue forget-me-nots sloppily
pulled; clusters thrown in

a messy pile. Eyes opened
by accident. Earth in the hair,

hair in the ground. Gentle
shoots blindly searching

for a creek, and fingers
feeling out the path.

This is the place where
sunspots are death spots.

THE FACE OF THE HUNTER

Day duration has increased.
A spider has been connecting

sweaty leaves with suspension
bridges for an eternity. When

the night came, dew stringed
water drops on the web. In every

little rosary bead—revealed
by enlightenment—there was

a reflection of the face of the hunter
hidden at the center of the net.

THE ASSUMPTION

On the ground that the young snow
just covered with a layer of white

powder, a series of small arrows
points in the direction opposite to

the direction of the bird's jumping.
The trail which seems to come from

nowhere, suddenly disappears, replaced
by two four-pointed imprints, like

X chromosomes. After the battle of
the invisible with the invisible, there is

no bloody trace of an assumption into
heaven: the wings of an owl fly silently.

FOR ETERNITY

As I slept in purple
carob pods, and while

still being the glue for
mummy bandages

conceived for eternity
—the sky was above

in a simpler way than
it is now, and the old

sun was letting off
more planets. It was

much easier to say
—goodbye.

OPENING THE EYES

We have developed color
for those who needed darkness

to flourish. They have given
the benefit of deadheading

to us who needed the night to
branch out. We sowed the fields

with devil's thorns for those
who could no longer bear birth.

To us hiding in the bushes—
they have opened doll's eyes.

HORIZON

There is nothing capable of
swallowing up our time

any more. Sacred cows' rumen
leather nailed to the edges

of black holes to stop gushing
winds. Two dimensions are

all we have now. I will never
lose sight of you again.

What appears on the event
Horizon—remains there.

THE ECONOMY OF BEAUTY

The soul of the oak blossoms
unnoticed under the bark,

trapped in mistletoe that
lends it its face and white eyes

of blind berries. Love is the rhythm
of parallel growth: the parasitic

clinging of a form convulsed by
the urge of the species to which

it does not belong. The nature of
this relationship is artificial, like

everything else that cannot escape
the predatory economy of beauty.

THE END OF HISTORY

Rainforests bloom with red lips.
Monkeys kiss them: free will is

in the range of jumping from
one liana to another, and

happiness alternately dews,
drips, and pours on the interface

of petal and mucous membranes,
bark and fur. Torn trampolines

made of the leaves and skins
of flying squirrels eventually

stop telling history in
the drum language of the rain.

THE HERD

Rough tongues have licked
the sugar of their blood and

the salt of their sweat. Their
sun-tired meat has left a square

of skin on each thorn.
We have been eating them

as we would eat ourselves.
These cattle—their skinny

ribs sticking out—have been
hacking their way through

dust storms; rolling in the
dried-up riverbeds for eons.

EVICTION

As soon as it bites an apple
in bloom, and eats all its nuts

before they get a shell—paradise
loses its place in paradise, and

it is no longer a matter of our
Kind—it refers to every term

driven from itself, and to each
of the dimensions of a point

that leaves the coordinate
system of its sphere.

THE WIND OF EXPERIENCE

The frost stopped human
migration and when it finally

dawned on our other Earth,
it dawned once and for all: eyes

defended themselves from view
with closed lids, and foreheads

remained frowning in puddles
of molten silver. Luckily, we

brought along the wind of
experience, and it stayed in.

DOWNPOUR

It was not pouring outside,
but under the roof where

a thick rain of lime never
ceases to fall. Lying flat

like grass—the two of us
feed on lime. Footprints

on the doorstep, still
wet, and white, show

in which direction the day
escaped from our home.

CHILD

Just don't say you're scared
because phosphorus will

light me up too. Any position
I take up will be hostile:

each of my non-motions
will carry one child of

movement and give birth
to it—dumb in a field

of red cabbage with no
beginning and no end.

FALSE THOUGHT

When growing crowded,
hazelwort flowers, otherwise

barely noticeable, empower
each other and disperse

butterflies with the smell
of shy purple. Their young

leaves, hiding beneath the
dried leaves of the beech

tree, emerged from the forest
on the clearing and conquered it.

The invasion had found me
immobile: comforted by

the thought that I was paddling
across the lake with water lilies.

DEAF MINE

I'm feeding the cold
chimney with juniper

berries and the waste
hair of a tiny old lady

with brittle bones and
her mouth set in a straight

line. Smoke without fire
is smothering copper

plates, bird droppings,
hollow shells, duck

eggs; sawdust snowing
from the ceiling. A deaf

mine is being silent
below the doorstep:

my window gets
shattered by the dark

cone of a tree, the smell
of spruce, and the night.

WHERE WE ARE

One day we hitched up
the team of our faithful

dragonflies and set off on
the paths of eagle ferns. Soon

we were stuck in a resin lake
and left behind where we were.

Homeland has since been a
magical place to talk to beasts

who, led by our example, eagerly
await the amber-colored dawn.

PUTTING FULL STOPS

The inorganic of our organs
irradiates with cobalt blue

the plantation of yellow raspberries
grown just for joy. For nights

and days, the soul squeezed into
the flycatcher's jaw, pisses yellow

on the landscape, and fly
agarics are getting strewn with

white dots: putting full stops at
the end of our inarticulate sentences.

THE FEAR OF PEOPLE

A potato man picked up
from the marketplace,

a pair of mandrakes
hugging each other and

the lockpick root anointed
with fern oil that makes

the door to my place open
by itself. All that underworld,

soiled with earth and drunk
on air, seeks its space in mine.

BLACK FURROWS

We will be able to fit into
a pack of Illyrian irises

only when in death we
rise from the black furrows

rendered by thunder.
The dark blue sky will flutter

like a flag. It will be our
new banner. The twin

stars will rotate around
the common center of mass.

Naked mole-rats will become
immortal holding on to our root.

STUNNED BY THE SUN

Every time it throws itself
out of the window, suddenly

and without twilight, opening
the petals of the flower carcasses,

the sun finds them in the same
place in the yard, their mouth

full. With a smile, they show
their teeth reddened by the betel

nut juice, and continue to chew
as if they were not already fed

to death. They just stretch
gently; never take off.

WIND ROSE

Every place has its wind rose,
and that rose, like every other,

loves blood, and that blood
becomes drier with each blow,

and every twelve seconds,
in a new burst of air,

a red powder ball falls into
the humus. There's a difference

between the apparent wind
and the true wind direction:

one is indicated by a needle
and the other by a thorn.

HAT'S FEATHER

If I knew how to keep quiet
they wouldn't point a finger

at me: I would be a fawn in
the bush, not a feather of

a blue jay on a hat. They
asked, so I had to say whose

hollow bones, played by
the storm, sound better than

an old dogwood cut with
a shepherd's knife into a flute.

GEOMETRY OF THE NIGHT

There is a dark angle in
the geometry of the night,

and I stick to it blindly
because my light has a shape

only when darkness
outlines it. I'm not going

anywhere except where
the black seed of the white

devil's snare and the smell of
the desert lily take me.

TOGETHER

Like dissolves like: fingers in
fingers. Chewed up under water—

herbs give off their odorless souls,
and no doubt, the end has come:

methane bubbles are freezing
on the surface of our lake.

Jumping from one to the other—
we move on together. The last

remaining path of solidified gas
is set off by the polar lights.

ICE AGE

When words run out,
a solitary breath will

sing an infectious tune
of laughter, and so will

the era of unlearning
begin; the epoch of

shifting responsibility
from the language and

its grammar to the waves
of sound spreading

muffled shots through
the ocean's icy sheets.

SLOW MELTING

Do it now because I won't
wait until tomorrow: sew me

a raincoat made of grass,
and put it over my shoulders

—wet and heavy. Let it drain
from me, let it drip slowly like

the sweet tears of slow-melting
glaciers that remain for a long

time on the surface unmixed
with the salt of the depths of

the sea. You row in vain:
the vertical of water pulls us.

DIM LIGHT

Under the wind, in the shadow,
under the moss pointing to

the side of the world that is
no longer the landmark for

movement. Where would you go
if you left home? Metal globes:

scorched planets thrown by
a trebuchet. This flat universe

shined with orbs of dim light
conserves energy for the fruit.

OBLIVION

I do not know why crows
lay green eggs, or why this

purple thimble-flower in bloom,
suddenly turns its head from me:

it doesn't remember anything.
Maybe I, maybe someone else

brought the seeds from
the edge of the evergreen

mountain to the garden and
let them grow in the semi-shade

of the ruined century for too long.
Maybe I, maybe the crows

had been feeding worms to
the beaks of cracked brown fruits.

BREATH-FORMS

Everything the starflower
whispers to me as it rubs

its bristles against my cheek
—I forget instantly. Anything

but the whisper itself.
I build breath-forms on

my ear following the rhythm
of the exhalation, and I firmly

believe in these forms: from
the ground up to the roof.

I attribute sky-blue specters
to the beaten black

earth and wet clay soils—
the only real material.

MONEY

Ever since I felt the loneliness in
the bone structure of the landscape

we walk together, I've been saving
strength, transparent as confidence,

dry as coughing, round as a full
moon, and silver as money in your

pocket. It darkened: my inner light
took on a clearer outline. When

the time comes, I will be the coin
to pay for our shared eternity.

EAR TO THE HEART

Peacocks, you scream in vain!
I put my ear to the heart of

the old wind: the rhythm was
steady and calm. The boughs

lopped off with a terrible crash,
and all that heavy breathing

between the cyclopic cliffs going
chest to chest with each other—

it was all fake. On one species leaf,
an image of another appeared.

THE POINT OF DESPAIR

The white night lets light
through the hole geometry

on the hat of the morel
that has long outgrown

the spruce below which
it grew. This rocket-like

shape is directed toward
the center of our Milky Way.

We go without going
time and time again:

straight into the refection
of the point of despair.

BRING BACK THE BLUSH

I remember the day when it was no longer
possible to hang things on the wall, when

the nails refused to obey orders, laid down
on the ground, and covered their heads

with earth. Since then, their only job is
to change the color of hydrangeas and

the eyes of sleeping children to blue.
I promise I will peel the seven barks off

with my bare fingernails, pour quicklime
over memories and sit in the ashes.

I'll do everything—and you? You just
bring the blush back to the cold cheeks.

I'M SORRY

Show me your wounds,
my golden chain tree,

so I can dip a finger in them.
Sorry, I can't release you,

but I promise I'll be a horse
in your mill. I'll get down

on all fours and rub my
knees raw from crawling in

circles around your miracle
—once I'm convinced of it.

JUMPING OUT

Discerning, making out, quivering:
the outlines in the dark start to

think independently, finding a gap
and a hole and a window on which

the embrace of the flesh still floats,
and a breath still talks to

the mouthless breath, and a hand
still waves to the armless hand.

Line by line: smoke bars. Fire crackling,
papers flapping. An eye following

another eye as it tracks the shapes
in flame. Jumping out of frame.

PALM LEAVES

As the intestines roll on the tip
of the spear, the swords cut

the knots, and life goes back
so fast that it is no longer possible

to follow the meaning of the words
written in the palm leaf notebook,

the wind says: stop me
and every swirl of dust stops, and

every grain becomes free: every
single dust mote touching down

finds the feet to run on the earth,
a howl for the mouth and the eyes

to bid farewell to another pair of
eyes calmly watching what is going on.

SMILING ASLEEP

I

The tip of his forefinger, first licked
then stuck into the thin air to test for

wind direction—its skin discolored
to the shade of purple—an indicator

of mountain sickness Socrates developed
while crossing over and rising above

the naked bone-white limestone mount
draped in pale colors of an early twilight.

II
Cured by the god of Epidaurus
but never raised from the dead,

Socrates is brought to a strange realm
of light. His fellow-possessed,

the scapegoat adorned with the string
of black figs and pelted with flesh eating

berries, is first taken around the city,
then hurled from the cliff into the sea.

III

His sparkling black soul brightens up
finding itself somewhere in the galaxy

of foreign stars, at the tip of the red-giant
branch, just one little moment before

helium ignition. Socrates, the cupbearer
of a brand-new god, smiling asleep,

his soul upon his lips; silver leafcutter
bees sealing his mouth with bitter honey.

STONE CHILDREN

Coliseum-ivy inserts old seeds
into every gap of time. That way

the lavender color can climb
high to the spot at the top of

the tower where the deadbeat
sky planted its chipped teeth.

The Mother of Thousands kisses
the rock with her green lips:

stone children keep mum about
frogs weeping through their skin.

CURIOSITY

We followed mindlessly
the trajectory of seed dispersal

from a poisonous pea seedling.
Stopped off in a race, paralyzed

by scorpion yellow in the grass,
we stayed where the curiosity

we call our mission sent us.
How to justify our immobility

now that the tear glands
have lost their purpose;

now that the best we can do
is run without looking back?

FORM-IN-ABANDONMENT

When infinity burns,
all the bodies sweat with

the smell of mercury,
but no one had felt it yet.

None among us: only
the souls who begged

every single muscle of
the form-in-abandonment

to relax like viscous rubber
and to release them.

Notched bark and peeled skin:
white latex binds two worlds.

GREEN WALNUT

If necessary, we will lie hidden
for years, like a bundle of dry

sweet-scented bedstraw—
the smell of mown hay in our

nostrils. We will hide in the shell
of a young walnut and pray

that it remains green for as long
as possible, and when it is ripe,

that the truth will not strike a
hammer blow, as a human would do,

but that it will separate the halves
with bare hands like an animal.

WOLFSBANE

Purple and blue are spilled as far as
the eye can see. It won't be long

before the dark matter bonanza
blackens my view. I'll stand still

and think that an unknown gravity
field is pulling me into the distance,

and that the new propulsion engine
is humming like a hummingbird.

Everything I hear—I hear like something
already heard. I have a name ready

for everything to come. I grow up as a
wolfsbane among the bare rocks.

UPTURNED SKIN

Ever since they forbade me
to speak the language of angels

—I refuse to laugh together with
those who emboss their wings

in the snow by waving their
arms. Everything is fine as long as,

trapped in the ice, fear is afraid
of its own reflection. I step

cautiously: the soft paw of a Fox
touches my feet. I don't know if

she's outside and I'm inside. The truth
just flipped its skin upside down.

THE CELESTIAL TREE

The celestial tree does not
release one leaf at a time:

when the cold breath sends
a death signal, all the gold

is lowered to the ground
like a girl's hair cut with

a Japanese sword.
The high treetop measures

the height of the sky, so
it seems that what has

started abruptly, is going on
for an awfully long time.

LUNA MOTHS

We hurt, grown like nails
into the flesh of the earth.

Our souls calloused—we
nourish dreams with the pus

of our hands, with the sweat
of our fears; with the cross

on our lips; with the seeds from
a henbane bell; with the eyes of

an owl on the wing of a butterfly.
Luna moths spread the pollen

of false hope and the dust of
empty faith around the world.

NAKED LADY

The werewolf of the rebellion
banishes the lean naked He-bear

from paradise. From now on,
my shoes are beast fleece

trimmed with sheep scissors.
From now on, my nails are beast

claws trimmed with sickle.
There is blood from bear canines

on my teeth. Everything is mine:
his brown fur, and his naked strength.

BLANK SLATE

Spirits accumulate points
into swarms and flocks, and

from them create outlines of
characters that anyone can

recognize without a hitch.
They fill the sky from beginning

to end. Even where it seems to
be a blank slate, there is some

aching Being that shines a light
from what it is no longer.

Absence is the most visible
phenomenon in this world.

THE HAPPY PLANT

When you ask what it is, they
readily tell you—red resin—

but the happy plant has long since
replaced the narrow leaves with

fingers: one drop of dragon's
blood on each finger cushion.

She does not fight as She has fought
before, and She does not need

the sky to fly. The earth is light
upon Her; lighter than air.

HORROR PLANT

Evil souls divide the air
into cubic meters with

black sticks: one can no
longer breathe freely here.

Like wingless flies, birds
crawl into the tarry sky.

Hidden under my shirt,
Horror Plant expels fear

from my chest. My heart
is green: a clump of leaves

beating midnight. There is
no time except for giving up.

SUN STEALER

Noon pounding on my scalp:
I steal the sun from the shadows

as I run across the stubble:
beneath the dry stalks of grain

—the living ground drinks blood
from my feet, unshod and

black with dust, scorched mud,
and crushed mulberry berries.

Jackdaws follow my gaze:
where it wanders—there they land.

THE CHISEL OF SILENCE

The wind feels thrilled: stirred up
by the energy generated in the heat

between the palms of the hands,
it lifts up the enthusiasm. The only

thing I trust is the chisel of silence
which removes the shards of words

from me. The yellow flowers of
winter aconite shake the ice off

as they grow. Tertiary returns to
my soul: the joys are small again.

GOLDEN SHOWER

Today I drank warm milk
with some poison: yesterday

my goats were browsing from
the golden shower bushes.

The sky for planting hope
has become soft and light.

Grateful for the rain in free
fall, I bowed to the ground

and I bent my nausea into
the shape of a human embryo.

WHITE PHOSPHORUS

They wrapped my frozen gaze
in a transparent foil; pressed

blood and saliva on the lips of
the marble with my broken lip.

I inhaled the sharp flour: the angel
dust swirled covering my lashes

with white, and the pain was gone.
Each time I run away from

myself—I am white phosphorus—
glowing in the dark for hours on end.

DAISY HEADS

Love vine, goldthread, and
angel's hair—join forces to

conquer infields. A ball of
yellow thread unrolling:

woven by the sun, it inserts
its roots into the tender stem

of the mother of thyme taking
its breath away. It's down

the field path that they go next.
Daisy heads wear them like a crown.

MESSAGES OF HEAVEN

My prayer book is woven of straw:
words fall out through the holes.

The spider's flower draws them—innocent
of meaning—between its white thighs.

The messages of the sky tremble:
the blood of pleasure, tiny as rice

—marks the way. Only when the equinox
turns all white lilies into lipstick red

will I be sure which path to send
the words to where they came from.

WALLED UP

Stop, Five-fingered!
Get home, don't run wild

on the hills. I will raise you
as if you were mine:

I will give you a ladder
to climb like a yellow rose

over the walled windows.
When I put my hand on

the bare rock—you shall feel
my palm against yours,

and the eyes of the blind
stone shall be opened.

ETERNAL LOVE

When one pair of pale lips touches
the other pair of pale lips softening

the scream with a kiss; when love cuts
the ground from under our feet that

no longer walk on this Earth; when
the larvae of brightly colored butterflies

begin to dance in the white eyes all
around us, we'll hug each other tightly

and laugh like Siamese twins when they
wrap each other in the tissues of their lungs.

THE EXTINCTION OF LIGHT

I know you will protect
the baby's soft scalp, the live

pulse beneath the crust of
the sky stopped in motion;

prevent the extinction of light
in a cloud of interstellar dust;

you will catch the illusion of
the color of our blood in the mirror

of the space nebula. You will do
anything to make it look like it was

before, and I know: we will again
be convinced that we are alive.

LET'S GO HOME

A touch of the tongue—like a
flamingo in flight. The navel

determines the beginning and
end of the world. The umbilical

cord floats through the swamps
of passion, torn off by a bird's

beak, and the kiss of the hungry
fish moves the old float. Blue cloths

hang on the rope of the misty hills:
I am going back to my roots. The core

of my universe burns down to a lump
of dirty iron. Let's go home, love.

POISON

Wild boar offspring grow tusks,
bear cubs bite each other's ears

and children build doll houses under
the giant hogweed flowers. The scorching

sun burns through the fur and singes
bristles. Hands—playful and bare—

get blisters from the toxic sap. All living
things measure the growth of their infants

by the speed at which the poison rises
to the heart and the weeds to the sky.

THE GUARDIAN OF HAPPINESS

This night is a rabid dog dragging
along a fence with star-glazed eyes.

Bell ringers pop out of the bushes:
mad dogweed stems shake the bells

as if threatening. Seated face to face,
loving couples put hands on each other's

shoulders waiting for serenity to take
hold of them. They should not move an

inch. The guardian of their happiness
is trying to cough up an invisible bone.

DRUGGED

In the canopy of rainbow
trees, small mammals inhale

the mist of eucalyptus drops.
They scrape the trunk with

their thumbs, gently and slowly.
One by one, the colors appear

below the bark: red as rust,
yellow as the carpet of wattle

flowers, pink and blue as opal
ore. Trees lift their hands in glory.

THE THIRD EYE

The gooey seed of the savior
draws upon itself foreign

bodies that accidentally enter
sight, and it throws them out

in the same manner as the eye
might exude the speck of

sawdust together with a slimy
clary sage grain; in the same

manner one piece of crushed
egg shell might catch another.

The egg white of an anguished
morning opens the third eye:

I am not sure the sun is that
thing looking down upon me.

HUNDREDS OF YEARS

The tiny yellow flowers in my
hair indicate that I was sleeping

in the bushes again. My palms
smell like mustard. Hairy and black

stalks of the singers' plant dance
along an abandoned railroad line.

Don't tell me that is what loneliness
feels like, because you've been

saying the same thing for hundreds
of years—as the rails keep us going.

HORIZONTAL GROWTH

It's a lot easier for me now to realize
that the fatigue is pulling harder than

the river vortex, and that the water is
crystal clear because the whorled milfoi

absorbed all the evil from the bottom
—my feet tired of swimming entangled

in its tassels like a pair of dead bodies.
Only now, when I know I don't

need to root in the sludge in order to
survive, will I allow the current to tear me

apart, and I'll calmly continue to grow
horizontally from each shoot of myself.

ALONG THE ROAD

The moon horn pulled from between
the legs of Europe, sleeps tight tangled

in the branches. Who knows which way
we would have gotten to where we are,

had we not inserted coins for good luck
into the hollows of old plane trees

along the road? Who knows, if we were
to drag sacks full of hunger through

the same wasteland again, to which side of
the world would our young bodies bend?

SMOKE

You who have just started to walk
upright—you do not need a rope

to hang yourself: you need it to hope
for a fire as you make the bow drill

rubbing two sticks of poplar wood
together, searching the distance

with your evergreen eyes, certain
that the first one you see there

will know how to blow the smoke
of your confidence into flames.

MASKS

Sweet incense and blood, sweet
incense and sweet blood: tree

alleys go on forever. They are
followed by your view of things.

Reality varies as much as the gentle
wind can sway a leaf. The vulva of

this world separates the lips of illusion.
All your pleasure, and every pleasure

of every other creature, enters into it
hardened to pain. We know who

we are as long as the sticky resin
holds our masks on our faces.

OVER THE EDGE

Life goes on through the purple
veins under the pale, translucent

skin of those who know exactly
how to be born happy, how to

grow side by side like stalks of
white dittany on a slope bathed

in sunlight; how to descend a
mountain without stumbling and

how to lean their heads fearlessly
over the green edge of the abyss.

DESERT

My mother lies to me out of
love saying there is a secret

entrance to a field that makes
happiness happier—right here

by the canal where yellow flags
pull my feminine soul out of me

with the smell of iris. My father
walks through the dust: desperately

searching for me with a lyre. "Elysium
is a desert, run!" he says. "Someone

has stolen the root of the rainbow,
and your nails are black from digging."

OBEDIENCE

I do not want to talk about
the hands that have moved

the leaf of the obedient plant
to make room for the growth

of evil, because they are the same
pious hands that pray palms up

with the leaves of the prayer
grass as they pierce my tongue

with a slit of the greenheart
tree, and break into the mystery

of my body by turning the gear on
the spiny tail of the girdled lizard.

GLORY OF THE SNOW

A million-tooth wind swipes
the desolate plain blowing

white sheets of snow off
its surface. I hand over the battle

without a word. Flags of defeat
waving. The pheasant's eye

pierces the ice with blooms in
the color of wheat. The glory of

the snow six-pointed star gives
buds. Crystal air stings my lungs.

THE PATH OF NO RETURN

We'll walk across the water on
a blue lotus carpet one summer

day in the early afternoon. As we
walk, sharp-edged sun cubes will

roll over our eyes and we will no
longer know how to return. When

early in the morning, the white flesh
of the lotus fruit chases us from

our dreams along with the seeds—
we will no longer want to return.

WHAT IF?

Mormon-tea plant swept
its hair across the bare rock.

A big peacock butterfly
trembles tangled in thread.

When the full moon's light
falls on the invisible presence

of a drop of sweet juice, it will
become clear that what was

expected was already there.
What if I fell in love with fate?

IT FALLS

An unknown force uses
the tails of swallows to draw:

the whole vista is mottled with
lines of hunger, lines of escape.

Flies fly out of the spiral's eye:
their spots darken the orange sky.

Let's see who would dare to gut
the birds today; read the fate of

the world from their entrails?
No need to predict the night: it falls.

WAR

After a long and heavy rain,
the wolf-milk scatter puff-balls

across every old stump in the forest.
Bloodstream fungi, pink as udders

of young cows, and tiny as marbles
for the games of long-dead boys,

waited patiently in the dark for
the memory of the war to sprout

from their spores, so they could
slowly move in search of a new food.

EYES SHUT

Flushed blush on cheeks
and scraped knees: children

easily survive crashes and
rolling downhill. My brother

and I first met at a time
when we didn't yet know

what it means to clutch at
grass leaves over an abyss

full to the top with bone parts
that we are supposed to put

together into a recognizable
whole with our eyes shut.

WITNESSES

I am sad because I do not know
if you are a Syrian Christ thorn or

a jujube from the island where
I was born; a weeping willow or

the willow of Babylon. Will the eyes
of the witnesses distinguish the scarlet

from the purple when they are washed
in your leaves? Should I sprout up from

the water like the Euphrates poplar
or let my hair down the river of tears?

PUZZLE GAME

Medusa wet combs her hair
to remove petrified faces.

There is a rubble on the floor
from which we should urgently

do something new to repair
the damage. Too slow for this

task, we stretch out on all sides
like poisonous honey in the last

attempt to attach a piece of
ourselves to someone else's.

A BLOOD SPIRAL

I once leaned my wound
against a wound on

a dragon tree. The spiral
of our blood clotted

and fled into the gloom
like a galaxy fleeing

through a hole in the web
of space without time.

The past refused to
take me in its arms.

FIRE

The taste of bitterness ripples
our lips and every next word

is rounder, smoother than
the one we uttered a moment

ago: the newborn sound moves
beneath the eggshell. The sky

burns to the ground as a basket
of fear hums behind six locks

of silence. I call the night watch
and bring people together—

with the same ease with
which I collect firewood.

ENCOUNTER

I thought it was a whirl
of snow—that creature

covered in thick hair of
solitude, waving to me

with a cedar branch.
At night, it floated down

rivers like a log, and
in the daytime, it twisted

sapling trees apart on its
way toward the spot from

which one can best see
the futility of our encounter.

THE FAMILY

The father gently embraced
the curves of absinthe vapors

and peeled a black mold smile
off the icon with his chisel.

The mother drank wormwood
sap, breastfed the child with

bitter milk and dipped arrowheads
into the eyes of strawberry frogs.

The little one put the moon in
a sack, rolled it over her back, and

began to carry the burden of light
through a pitiless green paradise.

MAGICAL PLANT CHARACTERS

Acacia pycnantha 153
Achillea millefolium
Aconitum napellus
Acorus calamus
Actaea pachypoda
Adonis vernalis
Amanita muscaria
Amorphophallus titanum
Anastatica hierochuntica
Anguloa uniflora
Antirrhinum majus
Arctium lappa
Areca catechu
Arecaceae
Artemisia absinthium
Asarabacca
Asarum europaeum
Asplenium trichomanes
Aster amellus
Atropa belladonna

Bellis perennis
Betula
Borago officinalis
Brassica oleracea
Brugmansia suaveolens
Bryophyta

Caladium humboldtii Schott
Calathea makoyana
Carthamus tinctorius
Cassia fistula
Cedrus deodara

Centranthus ruber
Ceratonia siliqua
Chionodoxa
Chlorocardium rodiei
Cleome spinosa
Colchicum autumnale
Colocasia esculenta
Convolvulaceae
Cornus mas
Crataegus
Cuscuta epithymum
Cymbalaria muralis
Cynanchum vincetoxicum

Datura stramonium
Dictamnus albus
Digitalis purpurea
Dionaea muscipula
Dorema ammoniacum
Dracena draco
Dracena fragrans Massangeana
Dracena tamaranae
Dracula simia
Drakaea glyptodon

Ephedra fragilis
Epipremnum aureum
Eranthis hyemalis
Eryngium amethystinum
Eryngium campestre
Euphorbia caput-medusae
Euphorbia tirucalli

Fagus sylvatica
Ficus carica ssp. Caprificus

Galium odoratum
Galium verum
Gardenia jasminoides
Ginkgo biloba

Habenaria radiata
Hedera helix
Helianthus annuus
Helleborus niger ssp. macranthus
Helleborus orientalis
Heracleum mantegazzianum
Hesperocallis undulata
Hevea brasiliensis
Hippomane mancinella
Hydrangea arborescens

Ipomoea tricolor
Iris illyrica
Iris pseudacorus

Juglans major
Juniperus

Laburnum
Laburnum anagyroides Medik
Lavandula
Lonicera implexa Aiton
Lunaria annua
Lycogala epidendrum

Malus domestica
Mandragora officinarum
Maranta arundinacea
Maranta leuconeura
Morchella conica
Morus nigra
Myosotis
Myriophyllum spicatum
Myrthus

Nebula cannabis sativa
Nelumbo nucifera
Nepeta cataria
Nicotiana rustica
Nymphaea

Palicourea elata
Papaver somniferum
Phragmites
Physostegia virginiana
Picea
Pinus ponderosa
Plantago
Populus alba
Populus euphratica
Potentilla reptans
Prunus spinosa
Pteridium aquilinum

Quercus

Rhinanthus minor
Rhizophora mangle
Rubus
Rubus ellipticus

Salix babylonica
Salvia sclarea
Scopolia carniolica
Scutellaria lateriflora
Sisymbrium officinale
Solanum tuberosum
Sorbus aucuparia

Taxus baccata
Teucrium montanum
Thymus serpyllum
Tribulus terrestris
Trifolium pratense
Triticum
Tulipa

Vaccinium myrtillus

Ziziphus spina-christi

ABOUT SANDORF PASSAGE

SANDORF PASSAGE publishes work that creates a prismatic perspective on what it means to live in a globalized world. It is a home to writing inspired by both conflict zones and the dangers of complacency. All Sandorf Passage titles share in common how the biggest and most important ideas are best explored in the most personal and intimate of spaces.